DATE DUE

WEIRD
INVENTIONS
FOR YOUR HOME

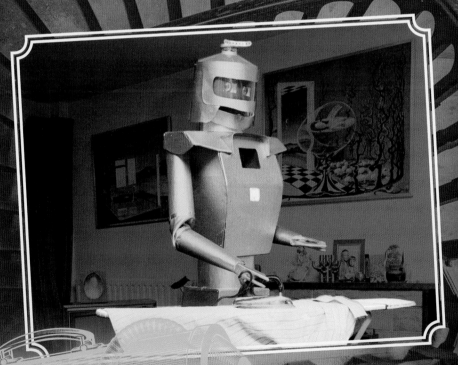

BY DANIEL R. FAUST

Gareth Stevens
PUBLISHING

Please visit our website, www.garethstevens.com. For a free color catalog of all our high-quality books, call toll free 1-800-542-2595 or fax 1-877-542-2596.

Library of Congress Cataloging-in-Publication Data

Names: Faust, Daniel R., author.
Title: Weird inventions for your home / Daniel R. Faust.
Description: New York : Gareth Stevens Publishing, [2019] | Series: Wild and wacky inventions | Includes bibliographical references and index.
Identifiers: LCCN 2018001276| ISBN 9781538220795 (library bound) | ISBN 9781538220818 (pbk.) | ISBN 9781538220825 (6 pack)
Subjects: LCSH: House furnishings–Technological innovations. | Implements, utensils, etc.–Technological innovations.
Classification: LCC TX311 .F399 2019 | DDC 645–dc23 LC record available at https://lccn.loc.gov/2018001276

First Edition

Published in 2019 by
Gareth Stevens Publishing
111 East 14th Street, Suite 349
New York, NY 10003

Designer: Sarah Liddell
Editor: Kate Mikoley

Photo credits: Cover, p. 1 (vacuum) AKaiser/Shutterstock.com; cover, p. 1 (robot) Fran Miller/Stringer/Hulton Archive/Getty Images; cover, p. 1 (key used throughout book) Hein Nouwens/Shutterstock.com; cover, background throughout book Creative Lab/Shutterstock.com; pp. 5, 7, 9, 11, 13, 15, 17, 19, 21, 23, 25, 27, 29 (hand used throughout) Helena Ohman/Shutterstock.com; pp. 5, 7, 9, 11, 13, 15, 17, 19, 21, 23, 25, 27, 29 (texture throughout) Alex Gontar/Shutterstock.com; p. 5 Everett Historical/Shutterstock.com; p. 7 Keystone-France/Contributor/Gamma-Keystone/Getty Images; p. 9 (watermelon) Koichi Kamoshida/Getty Images News/Getty Images; p. 9 (eggs) Michal and Yossi Rotem/Shutterstock.com; p. 13 David Becker/Stringer/Getty Images News/Getty Images; p. 15 Bettmann/Contributor/Bettmann/Getty Images; p. 17 (main) YOSHIKAZU TSUNO/Staff/AFP/Getty Images; pp. 17 (inset), 19, 25 (main) Fæ/Wikimedia Commons; p. 21 Barcroft/Contributor/Barcroft Media/Getty Images; p. 23 Alfred Eisenstaedt/Contributor/The LIFE Picture Collection/Getty Images; p. 25 (inset) Noodleki/Wikimedia Commons; p. 26 Tokumeigakarinoaoshima/Wikimedia Commons; p. 27 Keystone/Stringer/Hulton Archive/Getty Images; p. 29 ALPA PROD/Shutterstock.com.

Printed in the United States of America

CPSIA compliance information: Batch #CS18GS: For further information contact Gareth Stevens, New York, New York at 1-800-542-2595.

CONTENTS

Words in the glossary appear in **bold** type
the first time they are used in the text.

EASY LIVING

It's been said that necessity is the mother of invention. Many of the greatest inventions throughout history were **devised** to address an important need. The printing press, radio, and the internet all advanced the way we spread important ideas. Railroads, airplanes, and automobiles make traveling great distances easier. For every invention that improved society, there are others that are just plain weird.

When people think of time-saving inventions, they may think of ones in their home. Microwaves, washing machines, and vacuum cleaners were all invented to save time around the house. But, sometimes people can take the idea of easy living a little too far. From remote-controlled lawn mowers to tiny televisions you wear over your eyes, some home inventions are more wacky than helpful.

WACKY WONDERS

The inventor credited with the most patents is Shunpei Yamazaki. As of June 2016, he was credited with well over 11,000 patents in 10 countries!

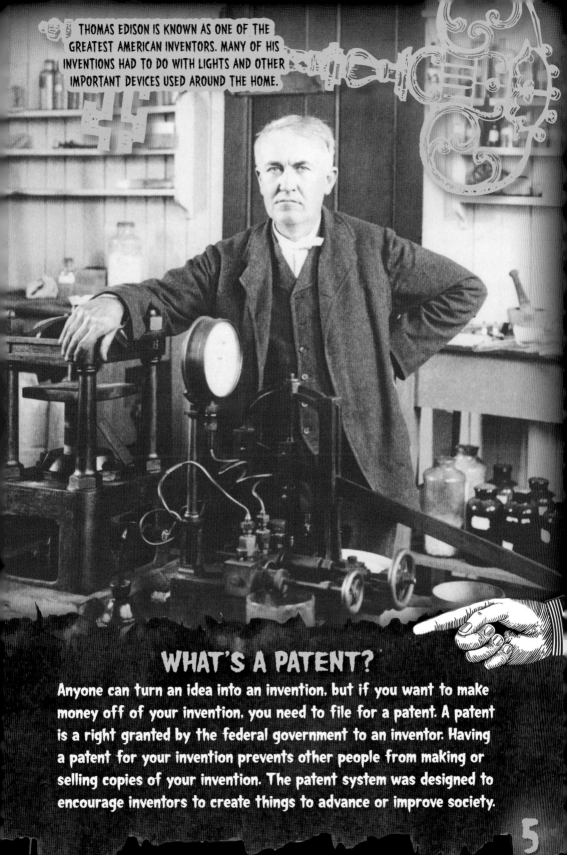

THOMAS EDISON IS KNOWN AS ONE OF THE GREATEST AMERICAN INVENTORS. MANY OF HIS INVENTIONS HAD TO DO WITH LIGHTS AND OTHER IMPORTANT DEVICES USED AROUND THE HOME.

WHAT'S A PATENT?

Anyone can turn an idea into an invention, but if you want to make money off of your invention, you need to file for a patent. A patent is a right granted by the federal government to an inventor. Having a patent for your invention prevents other people from making or selling copies of your invention. The patent system was designed to encourage inventors to create things to advance or improve society.

GARDEN GADGETS

Many homeowners will tell you that it takes a lot of time and hard work to maintain a lawn. Lawns require regular care, such as watering and mowing. Some adults might feel like they spend more time taking care of their lawn than enjoying it.

In the 1950s, more people were moving out of cities and settling in the **suburbs**. Housing developments popped up all over the country and many people now had their own lawn. Inventors started coming up with ideas to make taking care of your lawn easier. A radio-controlled lawn mower let you sit back and relax while you mowed your lawn! The radio-controlled lawn mower moved at about 2 miles (3 km) per hour.

WACKY WONDERS

Taking the idea of a radio-controlled lawn mower to the next level, there are now small robots that you can buy to cut your grass. They also remove snow!

THE POWER MOWER DELUXE

Called the "Power Mower of the Future," the Power Mower Deluxe was introduced in Port Washington, Wisconsin, in 1957. The rider sat inside a plastic case that was 5 feet (1.5 m) in diameter. It was air-conditioned and included a radio telephone and a system that provided cold drinks. The mower could mow, weed, and feed the lawn. It also could plant seeds and spray for insects. It could even be used as a snowplow and golf cart!

THE RADIO-CONTROLLED LAWN MOWER WAS FIRST SHOWN AT THE CHELSEA FLOWER SHOW IN LONDON, ENGLAND, IN 1959.

FREAKY FOOD

The kitchen is one area in the home where inventors really seem to go nuts. Many food-related inventions have dealt with preserving food or making it easier to prepare. In the 1960s, a company introduced pre-cooked bacon that was designed to be reheated in a toaster in just 90 seconds. Although a patent was filed, the product never made it to the public.

If bacon from a toaster isn't odd enough for you, there's another breakfast invention you might want to try: the Egg Cuber. The device is made of plastic and looks fairly simple. Just place a peeled, hard-boiled egg in the little container with the special "pressing plate," and screw it into position. After an hour in the refrigerator, your snack is a cube!

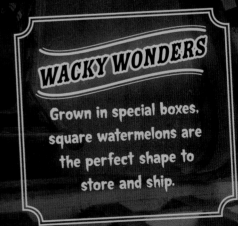

WACKY WONDERS

Grown in special boxes, square watermelons are the perfect shape to store and ship.

A BIRD'S-EYE VIEW OF FROZEN FOOD

In places where the climate is freezing cold, frozen food has always existed. However, the modern frozen foods you're likely familiar with haven't been around as long. In 1924, Clarence Birdseye invented a way to quickly freeze food. Freezing the food fast prevented ice crystals from forming. Such crystals would melt when the food was cooked and ruin its taste. Birdseye received 168 patents having to do with his quick-freezing method, including ones for special packaging.

THE KITCHEN OF TOMORROW

Instead of focusing on the food itself, some inventors have chosen to turn their attention to the room where the food is prepared. Over the years, a number of wild inventions have been made for the home kitchen.

As **technology** advanced and more people began to move into houses in the suburbs, more **revolutionary** ideas for kitchen layouts and appliances appeared. In the 1950s and 1960s, inventors designed model kitchens where appliances were hidden behind panels that could be activated with the press of a button. In 1953, General Electric invented a hanging mini-fridge that only took up half the space of a standard refrigerator. Creators claimed this model could still hold just as much as a full-size refrigerator.

WACKY WONDERS

The 1933 Chicago World's Fair included five "homes of tomorrow." They showed off some of the most modern features available at the time. These homes are now located in Indiana and can still be visited today!

WORLD'S FAIR

Many inventions first appeared at a world's fair. This is a large international **exhibition** focusing on a variety of industrial, scientific, and cultural items from different countries around the world. These fairs highlight and celebrate inventions and advancements. Many of the things that you would consider common were first exhibited at a world's fair. However, many other products shown at a world's fair never made it to store shelves.

FAMOUS INVENTIONS FROM THE WORLD'S FAIR

CRACKER JACK	CHICAGO, 1893
ZIPPER	CHICAGO, 1893
COFFEEMAKER	ST. LOUIS, 1904
DISHWASHER	ST. LOUIS, 1904
X-RAY MACHINE	ST. LOUIS, 1904
ELECTRICAL PLUG AND WALL OUTLET	ST. LOUIS, 1904
ROBOTS	NEW YORK, 1939
TELEVISION	NEW YORK, 1939
BELGIAN WAFFLES	NEW YORK, 1964
COLOR TELEVISION	NEW YORK, 1964
FORD MUSTANG	NEW YORK, 1964
JET PACKS	NEW YORK, 1964

INVENTIONS FROM AROUND THE WORLD ARE EXHIBITED AT WORLD'S FAIRS. SOME, LIKE ZIPPERS, TELEVISIONS, AND WALL OUTLETS HAVE BECOME EVERYDAY ITEMS. OTHERS, LIKE JET PACKS, HAVEN'T.

Designing new and **innovative** kitchens and kitchen appliances, or tools, didn't end with the 20th century. The digital age has led to the creation of new "smart kitchens." Many countertop appliances, such as coffeepots and microwaves, can be linked to smartphones or tablets and controlled and observed through an app. There's even a Bluetooth-connected **thermometer** that can check the temperature of two different dishes as they cook.

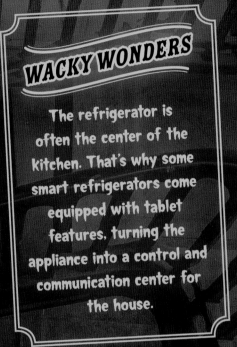

WACKY WONDERS

The refrigerator is often the center of the kitchen. That's why some smart refrigerators come equipped with tablet features, turning the appliance into a control and communication center for the house.

Smart refrigerators can do all sorts of amazing things. People can make sure their smart fridge is running correctly and check its contents over the internet. Some even have cameras so an owner can find out if they need to buy milk on the way home from school or work. Some smart refrigerators can even be used to order food!

SMART REFRIGERATORS CAN CONNECT TO THE INTERNET, JUST LIKE SMARTPHONES AND COMPUTERS.

CAN YOU TRUST YOUR APPLIANCES?

Living in the 21st century, it might feel like there's nothing technology can't do. Today, you can connect pretty much any appliance or device in your home to the internet. But, is this always safe? In 2015, security researchers found a way to possibly steal Google usernames and passwords through a smart refrigerator—and it wasn't the first time people found a way to **hack** into a smart fridge. Security is one of the major concerns with smart appliances.

INVENTIVE HOUSES

Imagine if the wildest invention in your house was the house itself! Many science-fiction tales tell about futuristic houses where everything is controlled by the press of a button or by a simple **verbal** command. Modern technology has turned science fiction into science fact! There are now ways for you to control the lighting, home security, home theater, heating, and air conditioning using an app on your smartphone or tablet.

If controlling your house with your smartphone doesn't interest you, how about a fold-out balcony? Built into a window frame, the motorized balcony can be lowered when you want to sit out in the sun or watch the people walking on the street below. The first model was mounted on an apartment building in the Netherlands.

WACKY WONDERS

A company is building floating houses off the coast of Dubai. The homes include an underwater bedroom with views of the surrounding sea life.

14

TODAY, IT'S POSSIBLE TO CONTROL ALMOST AN ENTIRE HOME WITH A SMARTPHONE OR TABLET. SOMETHING THAT SEEMED LIKE SCIENCE FICTION JUST A FEW YEARS AGO HAS BECOME A REALITY.

PORTABLE HOUSE, FUTURO II

THE INTERNET OF THINGS

You know what the internet is, but what is the "Internet of Things"? Most of us connect to the internet with our computers, tablets, or smartphones. Have you ever thought about connecting a car to the internet? The Internet of Things is the **network** of objects, such as cars or kitchen appliances, able to be monitored or controlled from a remote location, usually using an app on your phone, tablet, or computer.

15

LYING DOWN ON THE JOB

Even the wackiest inventions are usually meant to make our lives easier. Some of these inventions are quite practical and end up being helpful in many ways. Others might seem—at least to some people—like an excuse to be lazy.

After a long day, many people enjoy settling down by reading in bed. But, it can be hard to read in bed without hurting your neck. In 1936, Hamblin glasses were invented to allow people to read while lying on their back. The glasses used tiny mirrors to reflect the words from the page into the reader's eyes. The glasses didn't quite take off at the time, but modern versions can now be bought for reading and watching television.

WACKY WONDERS

Inventors have even come up with a bed that makes itself with just the touch of a button! So far, it's just a prototype, so for now you'll still have to keep making your bed yourself.

ROBOTS IN THE HOME

Household robots are robots that perform tasks around the home, such as cleaning. When we think of robots like these, we often think of them with arms, legs, and heads—like people! While some household robots certainly fit this picture, it's not always the case. In fact, household robots are much more common than you may realize. Today, robot vacuum cleaners can be found in many homes. They're usually disk shaped and use special sensors to move and clean around the home.

HAMBLIN GLASSES

WHEN PLACED A CERTAIN WAY, MIRRORS, SUCH AS THOSE IN HAMBLIN GLASSES, CAN HELP YOU SEE THINGS THAT AREN'T DIRECTLY IN FRONT OF YOU.

STRANGE PHONE CALLS

FaceTime and other kinds of video chatting are pretty common in the 21st century, but that wasn't always the case. Alexander Graham Bell patented the first telephone in 1876, and inventors have been trying to improve on it ever since.

In 1964, Bell Labs introduced the Picturephone. You could sit in a special booth and speak to someone in another booth while watching them on a small video screen. Booths were set up in New York City, Chicago, and Washington, DC. The Picturephone failed to catch on. Not only did it require special wiring instead of the existing network of telephone wires, but it was very expensive. A 3-minute call would cost between $16 and $27. That's more than $100 in today's money!

WACKY WONDERS

In 1964, there was a robot that could answer the telephone. Voicemail is probably more reliable.

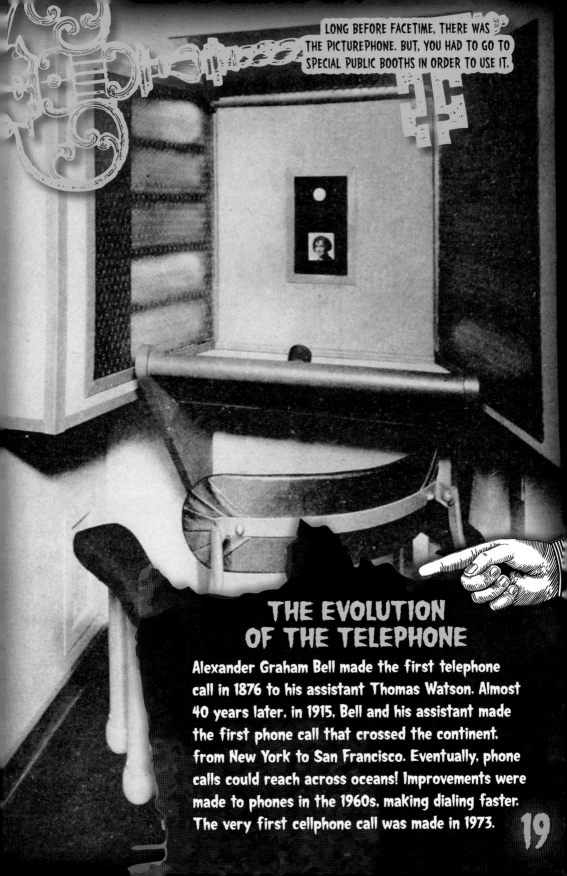

LONG BEFORE FACETIME, THERE WAS THE PICTUREPHONE. BUT, YOU HAD TO GO TO SPECIAL PUBLIC BOOTHS IN ORDER TO USE IT.

THE EVOLUTION OF THE TELEPHONE

Alexander Graham Bell made the first telephone call in 1876 to his assistant Thomas Watson. Almost 40 years later, in 1915, Bell and his assistant made the first phone call that crossed the continent, from New York to San Francisco. Eventually, phone calls could reach across oceans! Improvements were made to phones in the 1960s, making dialing faster. The very first cellphone call was made in 1973.

LOOKING GOOD

Beauty is in the eye of the beholder—or the eye of the inventor. We live in a society that places a great deal of importance on how we look. Whether or not this is fair, it's led to a lot of truly unique inventions.

In 1950, Ted Spence of the Los Angeles Brush Manufacturing Corporation showed off the Hairline Brush. The brush was designed to fit the shape of a bald man's head, with a part to brush the hair on the side and a felt pad to massage the exposed scalp. There also have been a number of haircutting gadgets invented that can be attached directly to a vacuum cleaner. This way, people can give themselves haircuts without worrying about the mess.

WACKY WONDERS

Brushing your teeth is an important part of looking and feeling good. One company has invented a bacon-flavored toothpaste!

THE McGREGOR REJUVENATOR

In 1932, M. E. Montrude Jr. filed a patent for the McGregor Rejuvenator. According to the patent, this huge device could reverse the aging process. A person would simply climb into the Rejuvenator, which enclosed the entire body except the head. Montrude claimed magnetism, radio waves, and infrared and ultraviolet light made the invention work. The inventor probably assumed every home would want one, but most McGregor Rejuvenators ended up in museums.

VALENTINO LoSAURO AND HIS
HAIRCUTTING "CLAWZ"

YOU CAN'T ALWAYS JUDGE AN INVENTION
BY ITS APPEARANCE. SOME MIGHT LOOK STRANGE,
BUT THEY MAY STILL GET THE JOB DONE.

21

ENTERTAINMENT OF THE FUTURE!

Today, thanks to the internet, Wi-Fi, smartphones, and tablets, information and entertainment are at your fingertips at any hour of the day or night. That hasn't always been the case. Before the internet, if you wanted to read the news, you'd have to go out and buy a newspaper or wait for your daily newspaper delivery.

In 1938, W. G. H. Finch invented a way for the newspaper to be broadcast over the radio into your home, where it would be printed. The newspaper would be transmitted between midnight and 6 o'clock in the morning, when most people were asleep and radio stations didn't broadcast much content. The receiver was noisy, however, and it took several hours to print a complete newspaper.

WACKY WONDERS

Although his newspaper transmitter didn't take off, W. G. H. Finch applied what he learned to an invention that would. In 1946, Finch invented the first color fax machine.

IN ADDITION TO THE TELEYEGLASSES, GERNSBACK ALSO HELD PATENTS FOR A LIGHT-UP MIRROR AND AN ELECTRIC HAIRBRUSH.

WEARABLE TELEVISION

Hugo Gernsback was an inventor and publisher. In 1908, he founded *Modern Electrics*, a magazine about the electronics industry. He is also sometimes known as "The Father of Science Fiction." As an inventor, Gernsback held around 80 patents. He came up with the "teleyeglasses." These were battery-powered goggles that held a pair of small television screens, one for each eye. Though it's said a prototype was built, the invention never went to production.

KEEPING IT CLEAN

In many homes, the bathroom is the smallest room. But, just because the bathroom is small doesn't mean it doesn't serve as a huge inspiration to inventors. Some inventions may seem obvious, like a hair dryer stand that lets you brush and style your hair with both hands, instead of using one to hold the hair dryer. Others are a little wackier.

Have you ever gotten out of a hot shower only to find the bathroom mirror all fogged up with **condensation**? Thankfully, someone invented a mirror wiper. It attaches to the mirror and you move it from side to side. It's sort of like a windshield wiper on a car. Someone else invented a pedal that lets you raise and lower the toilet seat with your foot!

WACKY WONDERS

Not everyone likes bath time. In the 1950s, there was a plastic brush that could be worn around a child's neck like a collar. It was meant to clean the neck without soap or water.

CHAMBER POT FROM THE 1800s

CRAPPER'S
Improved
Registered Ornamental
Flush-down W.C

High New Design Cast-iron Syphon Water
Waste Preventer.

No 518.
Improved Ornamental Flush-down W.C. Basin
(Registered No. 145273), Finished Mano-
gany Seat with flap, New cantilever design
Cast iron Syphon water waste preventer
Brass Flush...

FLUSH WITH IDEAS

A popular—but untrue—legend says an English plumber named Thomas Crapper invented the flushing toilet in the 1800s. In reality, Crapper's innovation was in marketing indoor plumbing. An early flushing toilet was invented in 1596 by Sir John Harington. Toilets like the ones you're used to using date back to at least 1775, when Alexander Cumming, a watchmaker and mathematician, patented the tool that made flushing the toilet possible.

25

In 1970, a German inventor designed the shower hood. The plastic hood slipped over the entire head to protect one's hair and makeup in the shower. It may have seemed like a good idea to someone, but it never really caught on.

Like something out of NASA, the space-saving "Swiss Army Bathroom" was designed with small bathrooms in mind. The single, narrow column stands 8 feet (2.4 m) tall and contains everything that you would find in an ordinary bathroom. The foundation includes a stationary toilet. The uppermost section includes two different shower heads. In between, you'll find a sink and various storage cabinets. Each section above the toilet turns out from the central column when needed and can be rotated back to the center to store when not in use.

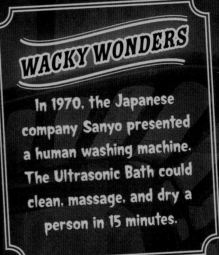

WACKY WONDERS

In 1970, the Japanese company Sanyo presented a human washing machine. The Ultrasonic Bath could clean, massage, and dry a person in 15 minutes.

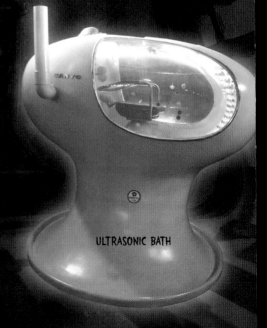

ULTRASONIC BATH

THE HISTORY OF TOILET PAPER

Toilet paper probably seems pretty common to you, doesn't it? Modern toilet paper was invented in 1857 by Joseph Gayetty, but it was sold in flat sheets. The Scott Paper Company first put toilet paper on rolls in 1890. Before that, there were some odd alternatives. The ancient Romans used a sponge on a stick. In the Middle Ages, commoners used straw, hay, or grass. Early Americans used corncobs, newspaper, or leaves.

SHOWER HOOD

SADLY, THE ULTRASONIC BATH, OR HUMAN WASHING MACHINE, NEVER FOUND ITS WAY INTO OUR BATHROOMS. LUCKILY, THE OLD-FASHIONED WAY OF BATHING ISN'T TOO DIFFICULT.

TODAY'S IDEAS, TOMORROW'S INVENTIONS

There have been some truly wild inventions over the years. Some have been really innovative. Others have been just plain weird. But as time goes on, and technology improves, the ideas are just going to get crazier! Many of the most successful inventions for the home are the ones that make things more convenient for people living their everyday lives. In 2017, the Ember mug was released. It uses special technology—and an app—to keep your drink the perfect temperature all day long. *Time* magazine named it one of the best inventions of 2017!

If you've been inspired by any of the strange inventions you've read about in this book, you might want to turn that inspiration into innovation. Remember, every invention began as an idea!

WACKY WONDERS

It may take a while for an idea to work. As technology improved, Lamarr and Antheil's idea did end up being important to the military—and to personal communication!

FROM ACTING TO INVENTING

Inventors come from all walks of life. Hedy Lamarr was a popular actress in the 1940s, but her contributions extended far beyond Hollywood. In 1942, during World War II, Lamarr and George Antheil patented an idea that involved changing radio frequencies to prevent enemies from decoding messages. At the time, existing technology was too limited to make the idea work. However, Lamarr and Antheil's "Secret Communication System" would become an important step in making the invention of cellphones possible.

GLOSSARY

condensation: small drops of water that form on a cold surface

devise: to plan or bring about

diameter: the distance from one side of a round object to another through its center

exhibition: an event at which objects are put out in a public space for people to look at

hack: to secretly get access to the files on a computer or network in order to get information or cause damage

innovative: having to do with a new idea, method, or device

network: a system of computers and other devices that are connected to each other

prototype: the first model on which later models are based

revolutionary: bringing about a major change

suburbs: a town or area where people live in houses near a larger city

technology: tools, machines, or ways to do things that use the latest discoveries to fix problems or meet needs

thermometer: a tool used for measuring temperature

verbal: relating to or consisting of words

FOR MORE INFORMATION

BOOKS

Higgins, Nadia. *The World's Oddest Inventions*. Mankato, MN: Capstone Press, 2015.

Meister, Cari. *Totally Amazing Facts About Outrageous Inventions*. North Mankato, MN: Capstone Press, 2015.

WEBSITES

Chicago World's Fair
www.american-historama.org/1881-1913-maturation-era/ chicago-world-fair.htm
This site includes a summary of the 1893 Chicago World's Fair, including maps and illustrations, as well as a list of interesting facts about the event.

Inventors—How to Become an Inventor
easyscienceforkids.com/all-about-inventors
This website has tons of tips to help you become an inventor!

INDEX